Penguins
Nature's Coolest Birds

Frankie Stout

PowerKiDS
press
New York

Published in 2009 by The Rosen Publishing Group, Inc.
29 East 21st Street, New York, NY 10010

First Edition

Editor: Nicole Pristash
Book Design: Kate Laczynski
Photo Researcher: Jessica Gerweck

Photo Credits: Cover, p. 1 © www.istockphoto.com/Jeff Goldman; pp. 5, 11, 13, 19 Shutterstock.com; p. 7 © Tim Brakefield/Superstock.com; p. 9 Age Fotostock; p. 15 © Getty Images, Inc.; p. 17 © Roland Seitre/Peter Arnold, Inc.; p. 21 © Fritz Poelking/Age fotostock.

Library of Congress Cataloging-in-Publication Data

Stout, Frankie.
  Penguins : nature's coolest birds / Frankie Stout. — 1st ed.
      p. cm. — (Things with wings)
  Includes index.
  ISBN 978-1-4042-4495-5 (library binding)
  1. Penguins—Juvenile literature. I. Title.
  QL696.S473S77 2009
  598.47—dc22
                                    2008003883

Manufactured in the United States of America

CONTENTS

Penguins Are Things with Wings

Have you ever seen a penguin? Maybe you have seen one at the zoo. Penguins are very interesting birds. There are around 17 species, or kinds, of penguins on Earth. All penguins live in the Southern **Hemisphere**, which is the half of the world that is south of the **equator**.

Penguins have wings, but they do not use their wings to fly. On land, penguins walk upright on their legs, as people do. Sometimes penguins get around by hopping from rock to rock.

There are many other fun facts about penguins. Let's learn more about one of nature's coolest birds!

Like most penguins in Antarctica, this penguin can move quickly by sliding on its stomach. The penguin is using its wings and feet to push itself along on the ice.

5

Black and White and Orange and Yellow

Penguins look very different from other types of birds. Most penguins have white fronts with black heads and backs. Other penguins have feathers of different colors.

The little penguin has a silvery, dark blue back. This penguin's face and neck are light gray and white. Little penguins are small, just like their name says. They weigh about 2 pounds (907 g) and are about 16 inches (41 cm) tall. The macaroni penguin has an orange, yellow, and black plumage. Its plumage is the group of feathers on top of its head. Some people think these feathers make it look very silly!

The macaroni penguin lives in Antarctica and on some islands off the coasts of South America and Africa. It is around 28 inches (71 cm) tall, and it weighs around 11 pounds (5 kg).

Feathered Flippers

A penguin has wings on the sides of its body, but it does not use its wings to fly. Instead, it uses its wings to swim. Penguins have to be good swimmers because they hunt for fish in the water. A penguin's wings are like a seal's **flippers**. Penguin wings can be called flippers, too.

Penguins use their powerful chest **muscles** to move their flippers. When swimming, penguins **flap** their wings. This makes them look like they are flying underwater! Penguins can also use their hard wings to keep themselves safe. They use their wings to hit other penguins that come too close.

The Humboldt penguin is a great swimmer. It lives on the rocky coasts of Peru and Chile. This Humboldt penguin is using its flippers to move through the water.

All-Weather Friends

Penguins live in both cold and warm weather. Some penguins live in Antarctica, where it is cold. These penguins have fat and feathers on their bodies to keep themselves warm in cold weather. Other penguins live in warmer parts of the world, such as Australia, New Zealand, and the Galápagos Islands. Most penguins live near coasts, where they can be close to the water.

The Galápagos penguin likes to nest in caves and on rocky coasts. It lives near the equator, where it is warm. These warm-weather penguins need to stay cool, though, so they have less fat and fewer feathers.

The Galápagos penguin is known for the white band that goes from its eyes to its chin. It also has a black band on its front.

The Lives of Penguins

Penguins use their bodies and voices to **communicate**. A penguin can make a sound and flap its wings to scare away **predators** from its eggs or its chicks. A penguin can even **recognize** the calls of other penguins and its babies. This makes it easier for a family of penguins to find each other.

Most penguins are social. This means they like to live in groups, called colonies. A penguin colony can have thousands of penguins in it. Sometimes penguins hunt for food in smaller groups. They dive into the sea together and help each other find food.

This is a colony of Gentoo penguins in South Georgia. South Georgia is an island between South America and Antarctica, in the Southern Atlantic Ocean.

13

Skilled Hunters

Penguins feed on animals that live in the water, such as fish, krill, and plankton. Krill are small shrimplike animals that live in the sea. Plankton are tiny plants and animals that float along in the water.

When a penguin is underwater looking for food, it cannot breathe, as fish can. Some penguins can hold their breath for a long time. However, after a while, they must come up for air. To get air, a penguin will swim to the top of the water and jump out. Then the penguin dives back into the water to look for more fish.

This Fiordland penguin, from New Zealand, is jumping quickly through the water. This type of penguin generally likes to hunt in waters that are shallow, or not deep.

15

Danger at Sea

A penguin's life is filled with danger. Seals, sharks, and many other animals **threaten** penguins. Leopard seals hunt for penguins in the water or near the edges of ice, where penguins live. A seal can easily hide in the water. Then the seal will surprise the penguin by jumping out of the water quickly.

Even other types of birds hunt penguins. The South Polar skua is a large bird that looks like a seagull. These birds eat penguin eggs and sometimes penguin chicks. Penguins try to guard their eggs and babies by making loud calls and flapping their wings.

Here you can see two skuas feeding on a penguin egg. Skuas are some of the most dangerous penguin predators.

Taking Care of the Chicks

A penguin's family is very important to a penguin. Both the mother and father penguins take great care of their babies before and after the babies are born.

Most species of penguins lay two eggs. The **male** and **female** penguins take turns keeping the eggs warm. When the babies **hatch**, the mother and father penguins take turns traveling to and from the sea. They bring food back with them, which they store in their mouths. The mother or father will then feed the food to the babies right from its mouth. The babies need this food to grow.

This Gentoo penguin is adding a stone to its nest to keep its egg safe. Gentoo penguins are known for taking great time and effort to guard their nests and eggs.

Emperor Penguins

The emperor penguin is the only type of penguin that **breeds** in Antarctica in the winter. The female emperor penguin lays one egg. Then she leaves for two months to get food, while the male takes care of the egg. The male stands with the egg on his feet, where it is kept warm by his stomach.

If it gets too cold, male emperor penguins stand together in large groups. This keeps the eggs even warmer. After 65 days, the eggs hatch. Around this time, the mother returns and the father gets food. Penguins work hard to keep their babies safe.

Emperor penguins keep a watchful eye on their chick as it grows. They work hard to keep their chick safe and keep it fed until it is big enough to take care of itself.

Penguins on our Earth

Penguins are very unique, or special, birds. Some penguins, though, need help because they are losing their homes and their food. These penguins are in danger of dying. Oil spills and damage made by humans are two reasons why penguins are in danger. Since penguins cannot fly, it is harder for them to get away from something that could hurt them. It is up to us to keep penguins safe.

The more we know about penguins, the more we can help them. Penguins are important to our Earth. We need to keep them safe so they can be around for a long time!

breeds (BREEDZ) Makes babies.

communicate (kuh-MYOO-nih-kayt) To share a feeling with another animal.

equator (ih-KWAY-tur) The imaginary line around Earth that makes it into two parts, northern and southern.

female (FEE-mayl) Having to do with women and girls.

flap (FLAP) To move up and down.

flippers (FLIH-perz) Wide, flat body parts that help animals swim.

hatch (HACH) To come out of an egg.

hemisphere (HEH-muh-sfeer) One half of Earth.

male (MAYL) Having to do with men and boys.

muscles (MUH-sulz) Parts of the body that make it move.

predators (PREH-duh-terz) Animals that kill other animals for food.

recognize (REH-kig-nyz) To know from past knowledge.

threaten (THREH-tun) To act like something will possibly cause hurt.

Due to the changing nature of Internet links, PowerKids Press has developed an online list of Web sites related to the subject of this book. This site is updated regularly. Please use this link to access the list:
www.powerkidslinks.com/wings/penguin/

WEB SITES